FREYA STARK
in Southern Arabia

THE ST ANTONY'S COLLEGE MIDDLE EAST ARCHIVES

FREYA STARK
in Southern Arabia

MALISE RUTHVEN

Garnet
PUBLISHING

Text copyright © 1995 Malise Ruthven
Photographs copyright © 1995 St Antony's College Middle East Centre
This edition © 1995 Garnet Publishing Ltd

First Edition

ISBN 1 85964 005 2

British Library Cataloguing-in-Publication Data
A catalogue record for this book is available from the British Library.

The photograph of Freya Stark on page 2 is reproduced courtesy of
John Murray (Publishers) Ltd, with grateful thanks.

The author would like to thank Hugh Leach OBE and Doreen Ingrams
for their advice and help in the preparation of this volume.

Frontispiece: Freya Stark with Harold Ingrams, Aden Protectorate, 1940.

Design by Paul Cooper
Cover design by Arthur op den Brouw
House editor Anna Watson
Reproduction by UDO, Bristol
Printed in the Lebanon

Published by Garnet Publishing Ltd
8 Southern Court, South Street
Reading, RG1 4QS, UK

CONTENTS

◆

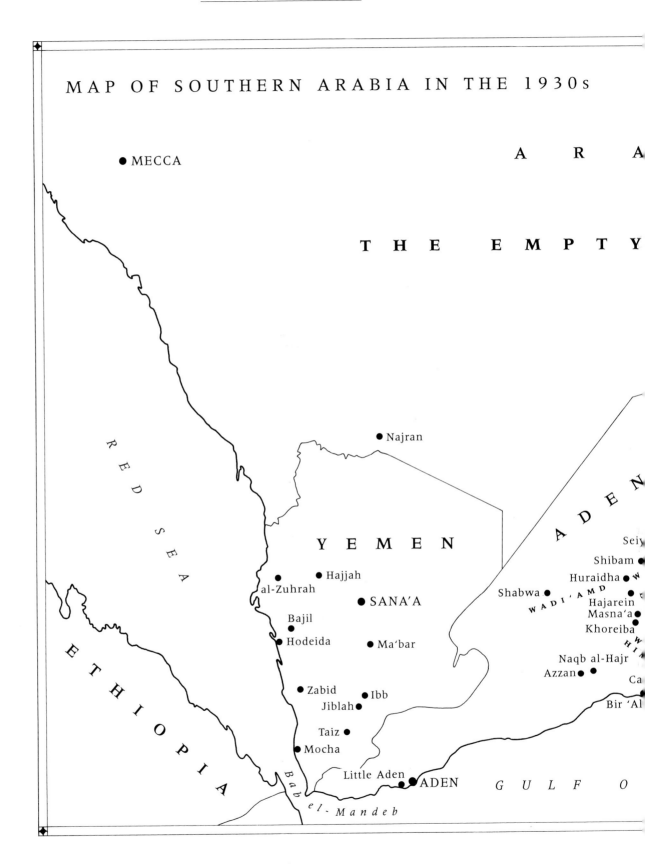

MAP OF SOUTHERN ARABIA IN THE 1930s

● MECCA

A R A

THE EMPTY

● Najran

RED SEA

Y E M E N

A D E N

● Hajjah   Seiy

al-Zuhrah   Shibam ●

Huraidha ● W

● SANA'A   Shabwa ● WADI 'AMD   Hajarein ●

Bajil   Masna'a ●

● Hodeida   ● Ma'bar   Khoreiba ●

HW

Naqb al-Hajr

● Zabid   ● Ibb   Azzan ●

Jiblah   Ca

Bir 'Al

Taiz ●

ETHIOPIA   ● Mocha

Little Aden   GULF O

Bab   ● ● ADEN

el-Mandeb

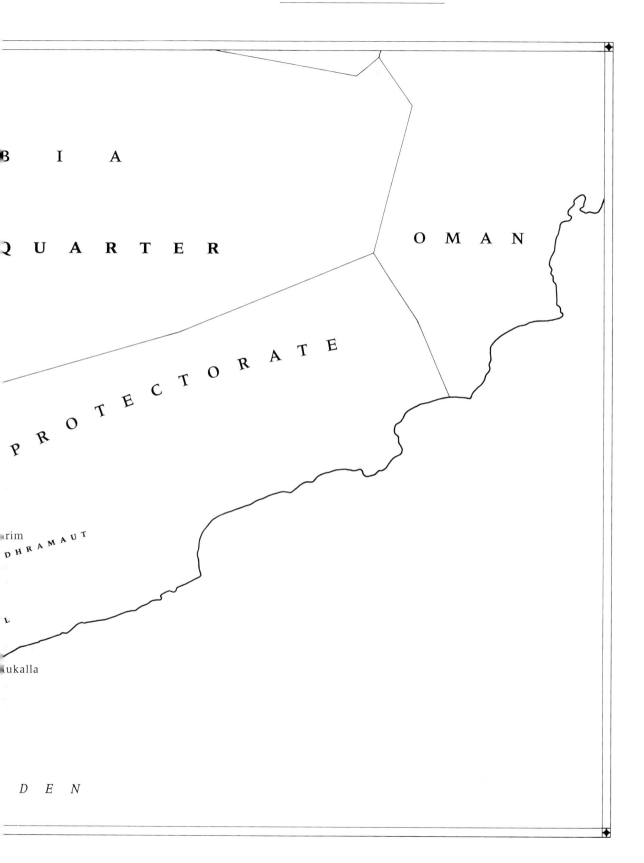

B I A

QUARTER

OMAN

PROTECTORATE

rim
DHRAMAUT

L

ukalla

D E N

INTRODUCTION

✦

The success of her travels in Persia, earning prestigious awards from the Royal Geographical and Royal Central Asian Societies, inspired Freya Stark to embark on new adventures. In 1934, at the age of 41, she set out to explore part of the Incense Road, stretching from South Arabia to the Mediterranean, which in ancient times had contributed to the fabulous wealth of Yemen – the Arabia Felix of the Romans. Though both Greeks and Romans forced their slave-driven galleys into the Red Sea with its perilous headwinds,

Approaching the Hadhramaut

they never succeeded in breaking the South Arabian monopoly over the traffic. Both frankincense and myrrh, widely used in religious ceremonies, are grown in southeast Arabia. Goods from India and further east arrived by slender, lateen-rigged dhows that were beached at Cana and other places on the coast to be carried by camel or donkey through the great canyons of the Wadi Hadhramaut, which stretches some 350 miles from west to south-east. Shabwa at the head of the valley was a major entrepôt. Reputed to be the capital of the famous Queen of Sheba it was known to the ancients as Sabota. According to Pliny it boasted sixty temples within its walls. From here the caravans headed north through Najran, a centre of Christianity before Islam, in what is now Saudi Arabia, and then east of Mecca (Ptolemy's Macorba) to Nabatean Petra and the Mediterranean. Though the South Arabian civilization declined, the traffic was never seriously interrupted until the Portuguese opened up the Indian Ocean to sturdier ocean-going vessels from Europe. By the 19th century Britain had replaced Portugal as the leading Indian Ocean power, forcing Arabia's coastal chiefs to abandon piracy and to keep other foreign powers at bay by signing treaties of protection. Relations between the tribes of the interior were barely affected. In the 1930s Aden Protectorate consisted of a patchwork of petty sultanates bound more or less tightly to the British government but internal strife was endemic. In the Hadhramaut the local quarrels of tribes and clans were fuelled by the broader struggle for supremacy between Qu'aiti and Kathiri sultanates. The Qu'aitis, who ruled from Mukalla over the seaboard and the western half of the valley, had close connections with India. Their Sultans were hereditary praetorians to India's wealthiest Muslim prince, the Nizam of Hyderabad, who recruited his bodyguards exclusively from among the Hadhramaut tribes. The Kathiris, who ruled from Seiyun over the eastern part of the interior, had links with Malaya and the Dutch East Indies. Many of their members were wealthy traders in Java and the Sultan lived entirely off rents from his properties in Singapore. Both were restricted from dealing with foreign powers other than Britain, represented by the colony in Aden, under treaties dating back to the 1880s. Traditionally feuds between the tribes had been settled by the Sayyids, an unarmed aristocracy claiming descent from the Prophet Muhammad. But with the spread of secular ideas from abroad the authority of the Sayyids was becoming frayed. Unable to settle disputes that were wrecking harvests and interfering with business, the chiefs appealed to the British to act as mediators.

The bearer of *Pax Britannica* was Harold Ingrams of the Colonial Office, who by his tireless efforts persuaded the tribes to sign a series of treaties that became known collectively as the *Sulh Ingram* (Ingram's Peace). By 1937 some 1400 separate tribal chiefs had pledged themselves to observe a three-year truce. Force was invoked as a last resort: recalcitrant clansmen who refused to enter the peace and continued to plunder their neighbours had their villages bombed by the RAF.

Freya set out on her journey at an auspicious time, with the prestige of British power behind her. She arrived in Aden with influential connections. She had a letter of recommendation to the Qu'aiti Governor of Mukalla from Lord Halifax, the Colonial Secretary (whose sister-in-law, Lady Iveagh, was a neighbour of her mother in Italy). She had two separate introductions to the legendary Antonin Besse, a dynamic Frenchman (and founder of St Antony's College, Oxford) who had lost – and regained – several fortunes in the South Arabian trade. More like a Medici than a modern shipping tycoon, his business empire extended from Somalia to the Hadhramaut valleys, exporting traditional goods such as hides, coffee, myrrh and frankincense, importing machinery, cars, radio goods, cigarettes and pharmaceuticals. Befriended by Besse, Freya avoided the somewhat tiresome attentions of British officialdom.

Antonin and Hilda Besse
with Arab servant

Freya's plan was to travel to Shabwa by way of the central Hadhramaut and then on to Najran and the coast. Shabwa was notorious for its hostility to foreigners, and had never been visited by Europeans. In the end Freya's ambition to consolidate her reputation as a traveller by being the first to enter the forbidden city was thwarted – as so often in her career – by illness. At the castle of Masna'a in the Wadi Du'an she ate with the women only to discover – too late – that one of the children had measles. Succumbing to fever, she spent a delirious week in the care of the ladies of the harem, who refused to let her wash, believing that soap was the cause of the disease. Though she resumed her journey she fell ill again at Shibam, and despite the ministrations of Mahmoud, an Afghan chemist summoned from Tarim, feared for her life. A message was sent to Aden and in due course an RAF bomber arrived which flew her to hospital. Before leaving she learned the bitter news that Hans Helfritz, a young German photographer, had reached the elusive Shabwa – though he had not been admitted, she believed, within its walls.

Freya returned to the Hadhramaut two years later, in the winter of 1937-8 with Gertrude Caton Thompson, an archaeologist, and Elinor Gardner, a geologist, who worked with her. Freya had been introduced to Miss Caton Thompson by Sir Sydney Cockerell, director of the Fitzwilliam Museum in Cambridge and an ardent admirer of Freya's writing. They decided to join forces for a dig largely financed by Lord Wakefield, a wealthy philanthropist. 'Caton' – as she was known to her friends – was as powerful, in her own way, as Freya, and it is perhaps not surprising that the initial attraction between the two women soon wore off. Tall and elegantly dressed, Caton was five years Freya's senior and had a distinguished record of digs in Malta, Egypt and Southern Africa. Unlike Freya she could speak and act with the confidence of one who had been profession-ally trained. She was no stranger to controversy. In Rhodesia she had scandalized the white settlers by endorsing the opinion of other archaeologists that the famous ruins of Zimbabwe had been produced by native Africans unassisted by more 'civilized' Semitic peoples from the north. The Wakefield expedition was expected to prove that there were no technical or cultural links between the ancient Sabaean culture of South Arabia and the Zimbabwe ruins.

Gertrude Caton Thompson

Freya's job was to handle relations with the local people, allowing the two scientists to go about their business without interruptions. But in Arabia, things were not to be so easily arranged. Freya annoyed the scientists by not taking sufficient account of the effects that Ramadan, the month of fasting, would have on the work. Feelings were further exacerbated by illnesses, born more stoically by the scientists than by Freya, who was again flown to Aden for treatment in one of Besse's planes.

Her talent for improvisation, one of her strengths as a traveller, was in-appropriate for a scientific expedition that depended on forward planning. On her previous journey she had inevitably been the centre of attention as travellers, male or female, usually were in the Muslim world. The presence of three *Feringhee* women, with their quantities of equipment, almost caused a riot. Caton requested Freya to "arrange things rather better, so as not to have a crowd". Freya replied that one cannot have the Hadhramaut without its inhabitants, "nor can one shoo these people away and still be welcome among them: the very corner-stone of their democracy is a general accessibility."

Matters came to a head when, tactlessly pushing a labourer aside in order to examine a find, Caton caused a fight to break out, ending with one man seriously injured. The argument was more than just a clash of personalities between two powerful women. For Freya fundamental questions of principle were involved. She perceived in Caton's single-minded pursuit of knowledge

an example of Western materialist arrogance: by giving science priority over human relations the archaeologists were exploiting the people of the valley. They were failing in their obligation to behave as guests. The fact that Caton was a woman doubtless made things worse. Freya was usually harsher in her judgements of women than of men. A male archaeologist would have been less threatening.

Caton surveying her workers.

Having confirmed Gertrude Caton Thompson's theories, the expedition broke up. Leaving the other women to return by car, Freya decided to explore the southern end of the Incense Road, making her way by camel through the Wadi 'Amd, a remote and secluded valley, to the ancient port of Cana, near modern Bir 'Ali. She was accompanied by Sayyid 'Ali, her guide, and Qasim, the cook. She considered the people of Wadi 'Amd to be lacking in beauty, with huge mouths, bony faces and eyes rather close together. At Zahir she fell sick again, but recovered enough to resume the journey through Wadi Shi'be, a narrow valley of scattered villages never previously visited by Europeans. Then they passed over the Jol to the oasis of Ye'beth, whose fortified dwellings were spread out in groups among dusty gardens and palm groves. At Naqb al-Hajr she was entertained by the Sultans of Azzan, anxious to demonstrate their friendship for the British – for as yet their territory lay outside the area of the *Sulh Ingram*. Here she joined a caravan of twenty-seven camels, admiring the way the Bedouins' few possessions, their water-skins and brass coffee pots, were perfectly adapted to this form of travel while modern gadgets, like her thermos flask and lunch basket, broke or proved too complicated to manage on a camel. After a few days they reached the sea and headed east for Bir 'Ali, trudging by night through a desolate landscape of grim volcanic forms. Here she eventually picked up the dhow which brought her, exhausted, back to Aden.

Freya returned to Aden within a month of the outbreak of war in September 1939 as an employee in the Ministry of Information. It was a happy time for her, despite anxieties she felt about her mother who remained in Italy. As a fluent Italian speaker who also knew Arabic, Freya was employed to counter Italian propaganda. Expecting that Italy would sooner or later join the war, she persuaded her superior, Stewart Perowne, and the Governor of Aden, Sir Bernard Reilly, to send her to Sana'a, the capital of Yemen, to counter Italian influence. With France (which controlled Djibouti) about to be neutralized and the Italians entrenched in Ethiopia and Somalia, an

Stewart Perowne with clerk

Italian take-over of Yemen would have left Aden dangerously isolated. The loss of Aden would have led to the closing of the Bab el-Mandeb straights, making the Red Sea into an Axis lake.

At that time the Kingdom of Yemen was still living in medieval isolation, virtually cut off from the outside world. The Imam Yahya, who had freed his country from the Ottoman Turks before the First World War, was an absolute monarch, who combined spiritual and secular authority as head of the Zaidi Shi'a sect. Embroiled as he was in frontier disputes with the Saudis in the North and the British in the South, it is hardly surprising that he looked to the Italians for assistance, although he also mistrusted them, especially after Mussolini had tried unsuccessfully to land troops at Hodeida, the main Yemeni port on the Red Sea. Thereafter Italian influence was exercised mainly through its medical missions and by handsome retainers paid to princes and ministers.

Freya arrived in Sana'a in February 1940 after a tortuous six-day journey by truck over "what nobody in England would call a road". Her entourage included a driver, a cook, her servant 'Isa, a mechanic and a technician to look after the portable film projector she had brought, along with several cans of newsreel sent from London. From her experiences in the Hadhramaut, Freya

Harold Ingrams (behind table in white head-dress) at a tribal surrender ceremony 1937

decided that the most fruitful approach to countering Italian influence lay through the harem. On grounds of propriety and diplomacy, there was no question of her meeting the Imam face to face. She organized a series of tea parties for the leading ladies of Sana'a, including the wife of the Foreign Minister, when she described the wonderful gadget she had brought with her. The display of images was forbidden on religious grounds and Freya made it clear to the ladies that she would not dream of showing her films without the Imam's permission. Within a few days a private showing had been arranged at the Minister's house, attended by one of the princes.

The newsreels, of British fighter planes and ships made a tremendous impression, especially as Freya had the sound turned up during the battle scenes. Prince Qasim talked about the "rule of the waves" for the rest of the evening. "But do not the Italians rule the Mediterranean?" he asked. Freya replied: "You would hardly call yourself a ruler in a house where someone else has both the front and back door keys." Word got about and soon the princesses were demanding to see the films. A showing was arranged in one of the Imam's palaces. Determined to find out if the Imam himself was watching, Freya deliberately blundered into the side of the darkened room reserved for men. As she suspected, she found him sitting there, surrounded by his sons. The glimpse was momentary as the princes immediately screened the patriarch away from the "horrid apparition" of an infidel woman. But the show was a triumph. The Italians were furious. When Italy entered the war on the side of Germany, Yemen remained neutral. Freya took a share of the credit, and her career as an official propagandist began to take off.

During her visit to Sana'a Freya took a large number of pictures. Most of the undeveloped rolls she sent back to Aden were "subtracted from the post and spoilt". The rest were destroyed by the captain of the ship which took her from Hodeida to Aden, under wartime security regulations. For some unaccountable reason Freya, who was proud of her record as a smuggler, had declared them and the captain was evidently a stickler for the rules.

Freya Stark in Thila 1976

The first shots in the expected war with Italy came while she was dining with Harold Ingrams. They watched an air-raid from his roof: ". . . eight beams of searchlight, and where they met, shining yellow in the moonlight, the little cross of the aeroplane . . . From behind the Crater, ball after ball was sent into the sky in long strips, like soap bubbles. It was all dream-like and incredibly beautiful, so one could think of nothing but that rapture of loveliness so near death." The next raid caught her out riding. She took refuge in a village police post "among Arabs, who take such things with perfect calm, only interrupted by delight when we seemed to register a shot". There were complaints from the garrison whose horses she borrowed and she was annoyed when Stewart Perowne forbade her to go out riding again. "I feel that every little crumb of beauty, every bit of normal, pleasant life must now be saved up," she wrote to Sir Sydney Cockerell. "One enjoys it more than ever in this black contrast, and perhaps that heightened sensitiveness is the greatest compensation in war."

Her friendship with Stewart blossomed, surviving Freya's transfer (against Stewart's wishes) to Cairo in the summer of 1940. It did not, however, survive their marriage, which took place in 1947. Unlike all of Stewart's English friends, she appears to have been unaware that he was homosexual. Stewart, it is generally assumed, thought that he had embarked on a *mariage blanche* with a kindred spirit, one that would further his career in the colonial service and provide companionship in old age. Freya apparently had very different ideas. Her bravado and romanticism, combined with a formidable intelligence, concealed huge areas of emotional naïveté. Her predicament was not helped by an adolescence spent mostly in Italy, which made her curiously innocent of

Freya Stark with Malise Ruthven in the garden of the villa Freia, Asolo, May 1984

those subtle British codes according to which important facts about a person's background or sexuality were deemed to be self-evident, and therefore left unsaid. The marriage was short and painful, and left scars that took many years to heal.

In 1976, aged 83, Freya returned to North Yemen after an absence of nearly 40 years. She made two visits as the guest of Hugh Leach, First Secretary at the British Embassy in Sana'a. She took lessons from a blind Yemeni youth to improve her Arabic, and took pleasure in identifying, and revisiting, places where she had been in 1940. Together they visited Taiz, and Mocha on the coast. Here they came to an old *burj* or tower used as a government guest-house, where she had spent a night during her journey from Aden to Sana'a. She told Leach a story that never appeared in

her memoirs, or published correspondence. As a guest of the town's governor, she had been given a comfortable bed, and was falling asleep when suddenly she saw a figure creeping into the room. Frozen with terror, she feigned sleep as the figure, which she had recognized as the governor himself, drew near and placed something cold and metallic against her face, before creeping out again. When she moved, the object suddenly burst into sound: it was a cylindrical music box. "I came nearer to losing my virtue that night than any time before or since," she told Leach, "including the nights I spent with Stewart."

ADEN AND
THE COAST

ADEN AND THE COAST

◆

The port of Aden is one of the world's finest naturally fortified harbours, protected from the Arabian mainland by the walls of an extinct volcano. It became a British colony in 1839 when the East India Company seized it from the Sultan of Lahej. With the coming of steamships and the opening of the Suez Canal it developed into one of the world's most important ports, commanding the entrance to the Red Sea and protecting the sea routes to India. As a coal store furnished with abundant supplies of fresh water it became a vital imperial asset, a "second Gibraltar". When Freya Stark arrived in 1934, the colony was still administered from India. It contained a cosmopolitan mix of peoples – Parsees and Hindus from India and Somalis from across the Straits, as well as Arabs from Yemen and the hinterland.

Freya stayed in the Arab quarter of the town with the wealthy Antonin Besse, "a Merchant in the style of the Arabian Nights or the Renaissance", "a wonderful person . . . who lets life play upon him as if he were an instrument responsive to its variations". On Christmas Day he took her for a moonlit trip round the bay in his launch. They passed "all the lights of Aden – people dancing in bungalows, sailors feasting on the ships" before rounding a headland where the

One of Antonin Besse's clerks in the Hadhramaut

shapes of bizarre volcanic rocks stood out against the stars. Besse enthusiastically endorsed Freya's plans to explore the Hadhramaut and visit Shabwa, offering help through his network of agents and contacts. Later on their relations cooled. Besse thought Freya insufficiently grateful for all his help.

Before venturing across the Jol or desert plateau to the Hadhramaut, Freya spent a week in Mukalla, the charming port that lies south of the valley, with its slightly dilapidated houses piled under harsh red cliffs. She stayed in the Qu'aiti Sultan's guest-house, where she was well looked after. While arranging her journey she took particular pleasure in watching the camel caravans arrive with loads of brushwood, accompanied by their Bedouin escorts. For her journey Freya chose donkeys rather than camels. Donkeys were faster, taking six days instead of eight and much more convenient for photography.

Salim

Originally Freya's party was to have consisted of two Bedouins from the Murshidi tribe and a ten-year-old belonging to one of them. Inevitably there were additions, as others attached themselves. One was a cousin of "sulky Byronic temper", who would wander off the beaten track or pull out a reed pipe from his loin cloth, walking ahead of the party, playing "monotonous wind-like beduin melodies". In addition, the Governor had insisted on providing Freya with a bodyguard whom she found officious and rather stupid. They set off on 21 January 1935. Their supplies, in addition to coffee and rice, included several live chickens to be consumed en route. They walked up the Wadi Himem "following, as it were, the work of water through millions of years". The arid immensity of the landscape was only occasionally relieved by small oases with palms and fields of maize. From there they climbed on to the Jol, a landscape which "gives one the feeling of being an insect running along till some huge crack in the world's surface stops it." After six days and nights, they arrived at the first of these cracks: the luscious Wadi Du'an.

Sa'id

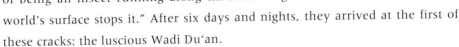

Government guard, Aden 1940

Government House, Aden 1934

TOP *Tea shop, Aden 1940*
BOTTOM *Harbour booths, Aden 1940*

TOP *A street in the Crater district, Aden 1940*
BOTTOM *Jews in Dhala, Aden Protectorate 1939*

LEFT *Guard, Aden 1940*
RIGHT *Guard, Aden 1938*

TOP *Ma'ala, Aden 1940*
BOTTOM *Aden harbour 1940*

Aden 1940

Aden Protectorate levies 1938

Nizami bodyguards, Mukalla 1935

TOP *Volcanic rocks, Little Aden 1940*
BOTTOM *Lighter from which Freya landed at Mukalla 1935*

TOP *South Arabian coast 1938*
BOTTOM *Mukalla 1935*

✦ 31 ✦

Mukalla 1935

Mukalla 1935

TOP   *West gate, Mukalla 1935*
BOTTOM   *Household well, Aden 1935*

Somali woman, Aden 1940

Water carriers 1938

Yaf'ei guard 1938

Khormaksar aerodrome, Aden 1938

TOP *Donkey caravan 1935*
BOTTOM Sikaya *on way from Mukalla 1935.* Sikayas *contain fresh water for travellers*

The Jol between Mukalla and the Wadi Du'an 1935

Freya's party approaching the Hadhramaut 1935

The way into the Hadhramaut 1938

THE WADI HADHRAMAUT

◆

THE WADI HADHRAMAUT

◆

The Hadhramaut valley, a vast funnel for the monsoon rains, inverts the usual geographical pattern. At its source near the Yemeni frontier, the river bed is more than forty miles wide. Before it reaches the sea it has narrowed to a gorge that is less than two hundred metres wide in places. The water supply guaranteed thousands of years of human settlement, though the quantities vary from one district to another. Some of the wells are 200 metres deep, and took months if not years to dig. Among the most distinctive features of the Wadi and its tributaries are the mud-brick cities that nestle beneath the canyon walls, surrounded by fields and palm groves. The dwellings, fortified singly or grouped together to form defensive walls, with carved wooden portals, attest to centuries of tribal feuding that interrupted business and agriculture. The lower storeys, which are without windows for added protection, were used for animals and storage. The mud-brick cities with their tall buildings have an astonishingly modern look. The double rows of windows on the upper levels add to the perpendicular effect, giving the appearance of skyscrapers. The designs and techniques of construction, however, stretch back to the ancient Himyaritic kingdom of the Sabaeans.

Before Freya Stark made her first visit in 1935 only a handful of European travellers had witnessed these medieval Manhattans. The first of them, Adolf von Wrede, an Arabic scholar who visited the area in 1843 disguised as an Egyptian, was lucky to escape with his life after being robbed of all his possessions. So far as is known, Freya was the third European woman to visit the Hadhramaut. In the 1930s the modern world

New, European-style palace of Sayyid Abu Bakr Al-Kaf in Seiyun

was beginning to intrude. Before the construction of the first motor road, vehicles owned by wealthy traders who made their money in Java or Singapore were carried in sections by camel across the Jol and reassembled in the valley. Radio sets brought news of the outside world, with bulletins eagerly transcribed into notebooks for wider circulation. The upper classes, like the al-Kaf Sayyids who looked after Freya in Seiyun and Tarim, were building suburban villas complete with swimming pools, electricity and telephones. Inside the city walls, however, the ancient sewage systems made the smells authentically medieval. Modern westernized costume had barely begun to appear.

Most of the pictures in the St Antony's collection date from Freya's second visit to the Hadhramaut with the Wakefield expedition, during the winter of 1937-8. Prevented by the fast of Ramadan from starting their dig, the party

Himyaritic inscriptions

spent ten days in Shibam, the most Manhattan-like of the cities. When they finally reached the archaeological site near Huraidha, Freya had plenty of time to wander about taking pictures of people and buildings. Particularly striking are her images of girls and women: the children in their festive finery, with plaits and jewellery and painted faces, the agricultural workers with their magnificent conical hats. Several rolls of film are given to the *'id al-adha*, the Feast of Sacrifice marking the climax of the Meccan pilgrimage, which occurred in February 1938. During the festival the people would visit the egg-shaped tombs of two local *walis* or saints, Habib 'Umar al-Attas and Habib Ahmed. After removing her shoes, Freya prepared to photograph one of the interiors. A Bedouin insisted that the saint would object. "That may be so," said Freya, "but do you think that your *Wali* cannot look after himself? If he dislikes being photographed, all he has to do is to spoil the picture." There are several exterior shots of the tombs but no interiors, not even a smudged impression. An unusually high proportion of the negatives are blank.

Wadi Du'an 1935

Camel men, Jol of ʿAmd 1938

Women wearing sun-hats 1935

Young Sayyid 1935

Bedouin of the Beni Himyar near Azzan 1938

TOP *Bedouin of the Beni Himyar near Azzan 1938*
BOTTOM *Bedouin, Seiyun 1935*

Children of the al-Kaf Sayyids, Huraidha 1938. Note the European jackets.

Girls in festive dress, Huraidha 1938

Girl made up for the 'id al-adha, Huraidha 1938. The paint on her forehead and cheeks was green.

The al-Kaf Sayyids, Seiyun 1935

The Mansab Hasan ibn Ahmed al-Attas of Huraidha (seated) and two of his retainers 1938

LEFT *Peasant woman winnowing 1938*
RIGHT *ibid. Some women used to keep dates in their sun-hats.*

Pupil, possibly Huraidha 1938

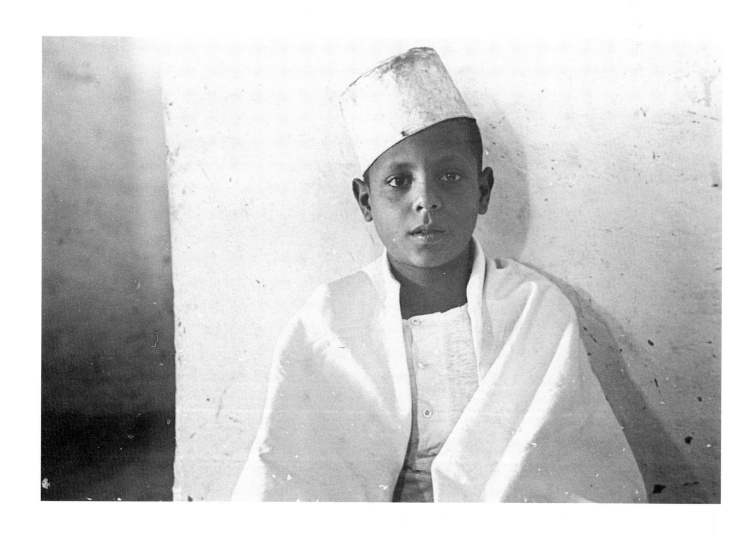

Young Sayyid, Huraidha 1938

The "old house" of Sayyid Abu Bakr al-Kaf in Seiyun. "The decoration is rather pretentious",
wrote Freya, "but the house in its garden of palm trees looks well."

Tarim 1935. The fluting on the lower walls is characteristic of this city.

Water jars, Tarim 1935

LEFT *Huraidha 1938*
RIGHT *Tarim 1935*

Sayyid Ba Surra standing on the roof of the al-Qatn mosque in the Wadi Du'an 1938

Scales, Huraidha 1938

Builder, Huraidha 1938

Pool in Sayyid Abu Bakr al-Kaf's garden, Seiyun 1938. The villa is now a secondary school.

Wadi Du'an 1935

Hajarein 1935

Yaf'ei guards, Shibam 1938

"Archaeology in the Hadhramaut" – *Elinor Gardner and Gertrude Caton Thompson* (ahead) *near Huraidha 1938*

TOP *Kathiri armed constabulary, Seiyun 1938*
BOTTOM *ibid.*

South gate, Tarim 1935

Khoreiba 1935

'Ali bin Mansour, Sultan of Seiyun 1935

Wedding crowd before the palace of Sayyid Abdul Rahman al-Kaf, Tarim 1935

'id al-kabir, *Shibam 1938*

Wedding, Hajarein 1935

'id al-kabir, *Shibam 1938*

'id al-adha *(Feast of Pilgrimage), Huraidha 1938*

'id al-adha *(Feast of Pilgrimage), Huraidha 1938*

'id al-adha *(Feast of Pilgrimage), Huraidha 1938*

TOP ´id al-adha *(Feast of Pilgrimage), Huraidha 1938*
BOTTOM *Shibam 1938*

Kathiri Sultan's palace, Seiyun 1935. The building had recently been whitewashed. Earlier travellers described it as having bands of whitewash against the brown mud-brick.

*Siesta under an 'ilb tree (*ficus salicifolia*) in the Wadi Rahbe 1938*

Ravines of Huraidha 1938

TOP *Pool of Bahr near Huraidha 1938*
BOTTOM *ʿAqabat al-Hibl (Pass of the Strings), leading into Wadi Duʿan 1935*

TOP *The* Wadi *near Azzan 1938. "The abundance of water must ever have made this a fertile region, but constant inter-tribal wars have kept it uncultivated of late."*
BOTTOM *Walls of Seiyun 1938*

Caravan's end: the coast near Bir 'Ali 1938

YEMEN

YEMEN

✦

Virtually all the pictures of Sana'a and the kingdom of Yemen that Freya took during her first visit in 1940 have been lost or were destroyed on the orders of the British captain who took her back to Aden in March 1940, a few weeks before Italy entered the Second World War. The photographs in this section all date from two visits she made in March and November 1976 as the guest of Hugh Leach, First Secretary at the British Embassy in Sana'a, "a new young friend who has made himself a garden with lawn and flowers in the old walls, and loves and knows the people." In Sana'a she wandered about the old city, trying to identify the houses where she had stayed. "So glad to see it all again," she wrote, "and apart from too many cars, not really different. The tall stone houses and their white painted windows are clustered just the same, and the crowd more friendly than 1940. I am so happy to see it all and had forgotten the incredible beauty." They drove to Taiz, the southern capital, climbing a 10,000-foot pass that gave her the chance to survey the landscape with its jagged peaks "like spears in motion" and compact rows of terracing built to catch the monsoon rains. "You look down into valleys lying about like

Private conversation 1976

cups filled to the brim with terraces of a drug called *qat*, which is the most precious plant they have. It is such a troublesome thing, and more so now than ever, to see so much labour given to tiny plots of earth." The driver, she noted, regularly stopped at a roadside shanty to buy a bunch of *qat*, a mild stimulant to which most Yemeni men are addicted. Near Ma'bar the Landrover broke down, and they had to complete their journey in the dark. Freya was unperturbed. "We had to sit by the road for five hours while they fixed the gearbox," Leach recalls. "At 83 she was remarkably uncomplaining, a wonderful traveller in that sense."

On her three week visit in November Freya spent her mornings in Hugh Leach's garden, improving her Arabic in conversation with Ahmed, a blind boy, in preparation for her forthcoming journey down the Euphrates (see

Preparing a shot 1936

Freya Stark in the Levant). She made trips to Thila and other towns within reach of the capital before setting off with Leach, his friend and colleague, John Shipman, and Mubarak, the driver, for a "safari" to the Tihama – the coastal plain. After making a northern loop through Bajil and al-Zuhrah to the mountain town of Hajjah, the party drove south to Jarahi, Mubarak's village near Zabid, where they attended the wedding of Mubarak's daughter. Unfortunately Freya's camera seized up near Hajjah, and there are no pictures of the wedding and '*id al-adha*' festival which coincided with it.

In the gentle temper of her old age Freya found the slaughter that accompanied these festivities overwhelming. "Both Hugh's friend and I collapsed under the strain of so many immolated kids and lambs and goats and I think seriously of becoming a vegetarian: all those patient little creatures taught to expect nothing but kindness from human beings and led off like the September Massacres with the mild eyes of their little groups following them into darkness. The little bride, too, just fourteen, was led in with her face covered and a brocade over her head and shoulders, the black veil all wet with tears and her fevered little hands limp when I pressed them. And yet the old women who survive it all have a wonderful serenity."

Thila, 25 miles north-west of Sana'a 1976

TOP *Himyaritic water cistern at Qal'at al-Khadhra, near Jiblah 1976*
BOTTOM *Women, Thila 1976*

TOP *Village store in the Haimatain west of Sana'a 1976*
BOTTOM *Villagers, Thila 1976*

Highlanders at Shibam, north-west of Sana'a 1976

TOP *View from Naqil Yislah, near Ma'bar on Sana'a–Taiz road 1976*
BOTTOM *Village and terracing at Haimatain 1976*

Suq al-Mu'arras in the Tihama coastal plain 1976

Woman, al-Haimat al-Dakhiliya, north-west of Sana'a 1976

TOP *Sana'a 1976*
BOTTOM *ibid*

Jiblah, north of Taiz 1976

Jiblah mosque 1976

Sana'a 1976

LEFT *Villager, Shibam 1976*
RIGHT *Sana'a street 1976*

Men of Thila 1976

Thila 1976

View of Beit Wazir from Jebel Sabir, near Taiz 1976

TOP *Village and terracing in al-Haimat al-Dakhiliya 1976*
BOTTOM *Terracing on the Jebel Sabir, near Taiz 1976. The terraces need constant maintenance. If they
are abandoned or neglected, the monsoon rains will quickly cause them to collapse.*

CHRONOLOGY

✦

1893	Born 31 January in Paris to Robert and Flora Stark.
1894	Sister Vera born.
1906	Loses part of her scalp in accident in Italian carpet factory.
1911	Enters Bedford College, London, boarding with Viva Jeyes. Meets Professor W. P. Ker who becomes her mentor. Robert Stark leaves his family and emigrates to Canada. Flora Stark remains in Italy.
1914	On the outbreak of war works briefly in the censorship department before volunteering as a nurse in G. M. Trevelyan's Italian ambulance unit.
1915	Serves in hospitals near Italian-Austrian front. Witnesses famous Italian retreat from Caporetto.
1921	Begins learning Arabic from her home at La Mortela near Genoa.
1923	Death of W. P. Ker while climbing with F.S. on Monte Rosa.
1926	Herbert Young, a friend of her father's, makes her his heir to the Casa Freia at Asolo, the Venetian hill town which becomes her home. Vera dies of septicaemia, following a miscarriage, leaving four young children.
1927	Enrols at the School of Oriental and African Studies in London to continue Arabic classes.
1927	December–March 1928. Spends winter in Broumana, near Beirut, improving Arabic.
1928	Visits Damascus. Expedition to Jebel Druze with Venetia Buddicom. Returns to Italy via Transjordan, Palestine and Egypt.
1929	Arrives in Baghdad.
1930–1	Visits Castles of the Assassins, and travels through Western Persia.
1932	*Baghdad Sketches* published by *Baghdad Times*.
1933	Travels in Persia earn the Royal Geographical Society's Back Memorial Grant.
1934	*Valley of the Assassins* published to critical acclaim. First journey to the Hadhramaut in South Arabia (now Yemen).
1936	*The Southern Gates of Arabia* published.
1938	Wakefield Expedition to Hadhramaut with archaeologist Gertrude Caton Thompson.
1939	April–May: visits Crusader Castles in Syria. September: sent to Aden as assistant to Stewart Perowne in Government Information Department.
1940	February: travels to Sana'a, the Yemeni capital, to counter pro-Axis influence. June: Italy enters war – Sana'a remains neutral. September: transferred to Cairo. October: *Winter in Arabia* published. December: begins work recruiting Egyptians for anti-Axis "Brotherhood of Freedom".
1941	Divides time between Cairo and Baghdad, where she establishes Iraqi branch of the Brotherhood. May: endures siege of British Embassy by nationalist government of Rashid Ali al Gailani. Remains mostly in Baghdad till July 1942.
1942	April: visits Northern Iraq and Iraqi Kurdistan. July–October: on leave in Cyprus. Encouraged by Sir Sidney Cockerell begins work on first volume of autobiography *Traveller's Prelude*. November: Flora Stark dies in the USA. *Letter from Syria*, based on 1927-8 travels in Levant, published. Receives Founder's Gold Medal from Royal Geographic Society for travels in South Arabia.
1943	February–March: Visits Wavells in India. Drives back through Persia, selling government car at considerable profit in Tehran. October–June 1944: tours USA to defend British policy of restricting Jewish immigration into Palestine.
1944	August–January 1945: stays in England, writing *East is West*.
1945	February: flies to India to work with Lady Wavell in mustering support for Empire among Indian women. 3 May VE Day. July: returns to Casa Freia in Asolo. Works for Ministry of Information setting up reading centres in Italy under auspices of Allied Military Government.

1947   October: marries Stewart Perowne.

1948   February: joins Perowne in Barbados, where he was Deputy Governor. July: returns to Italy and remains in Europe apart from visit to West Indies in December–March 1949. *Perseus in the Wind,* essays, published.

1950   March: joins Perowne in Libya where he has been appointed Adviser to new government of King Idris. *Traveller's Prelude* published. Visits Greece.

1951   March: returns to Asolo, deciding marriage is over. Honorary Degree from Glasgow University. *Beyond Euphrates* (autobiography vol. II), published.

1952   Marriage dissolved. Autumn: travels in Greece and Turkey.

1953   June: awarded CBE in Coronation Honours. *Coast of Incense* (autobiography vol. III) published.

1954   March–August: travels in Syria, Turkey and Greece. *Ionia: A Quest* published.

1956   May–July: visits "lost" Byzantine cities in Northern Syria and Southern Turkey. *The Lycian Shore* published.

1957   Autumn: visits Turkey, Mosul and Baghdad.

1958   July–August: visits Northern and Central Turkey. *Alexander's Path* published.

1959   Visits Iran, Greece, Lebanon and Kenya. *Riding to the Tigris* published.

1960   Visits Tunisia, Greece and Turkey

1961   Visits Cambodia, China, India, Turkey, Lebanon and Egypt. *Dust in the Lion's Paw* (autobiography vol. IV) published.

1962   Visits central Turkey.

1963   Visits Istanbul. *The Journey's Echo* – an anthology, published.

1964   Begins building Montoria, new house outside Asolo.

1966   Sells Casa Freia to Asolo municipality. Visits Greece and Turkey. *Rome on the Euphrates* published.

1967   September: visits Afghanistan, Samarkand, Bukhara and Tashkent.

1968   Visits Afghanistan and Greece. *The Zodiac Arch,* anthology, published.

1970   November: visits Nepal. *The Minaret of Djam* published.

1972   Becomes Dame of the British Empire in New Year's Honours.

1973   Sells Montoria, moves to flat in Asolo. Visits Kashmir.

1975   Visits Bodrum and Istanbul in Turkey.

1976   March: visits Sana'a, North Yemen and Southern Turkey. Stays with Queen Mother in Castle of Mey. *A Peak in Darien,* essays, published.

1977   To Syria with BBC television crew for journey down the Euphrates on specially constructed raft.

1984   Revisits Nepal with BBC television crew.

1985   Receives Freedom of the City of Asolo.

1993   31 January: celebrates 100th birthday. 9 May: dies at her home in Asolo.

All of Freya Stark's books are published by John Murray with the exception of eight volumes of letters edited by Lucy and Caroline Moorehead, published by Michael Russell between 1974 and 1982. A book of photographs of South Arabia, *Seen in the Hadhramaut,* appeared in 1938. *Over the Rim of the World,* a selection of letters edited by Caroline Moorehead, published by Murrays in association with Michael Russell, appeared in 1988. Books about Freya Stark include *A Tower in the Wall* by Alexander Maitland (Blackwood 1982), *Traveller Through Time* by Malise Ruthven (Viking 1986), *Freya Stark* by Caroline Moorehead (Penguin 1986) and *Freya Stark – a biography* by Molly Izzard (Hodder & Stoughton 1993).